Fortune Cookies

Volume 11

Dr. Kareem Pottinger

YSD Publishing House

Library of Congress Catalog in
Publication Data

YSD PUBLISHING HOUSE
14490 Coastal Bay Circle 13204
Naples, FL. 34119

Library of Congress Catalog Card
Number:
2013934185
International Standard Book
Number 978-1-937171-10-0

Dedicated to my firstborn

YOUNGSABATH POTTINGER

If I ever leave this planet, I have
always kept you in mind.

Not leavening my wisdom far behind

Grow Good

INTRODUCTION

The true intent of this book
was to write a set of guidelines
that could be
immediately implemented in
the progress and advancement
of my sons elite
life.
This vast deep knowledge was
to be used as a
tool
to keep him far beyond just,
"ahead of the learning curb" for
lack of better expression.
These
rules are the widely accepted
and used unspoken
secrets amongst the elite in
which we use to rear our

young.
Although these are our
secrets
and most of us will and should
be extremely displeased for
having them on display for the
"normal's" of the world to
receive, I decided to release
them nevertheless.
For,
upon reading the finished
piece I realized that these elite
secrets
could not only serve to benefit
my son and family to come
well, but that the entire
world
could serve to benefit from
these lists of guidelines.
The way that this book is
intended to be received is to

ponder upon each page for a complete 24 hours.
Each page is to be pondered upon for the whole day; it is to be used as topic of discussion for that day amongst peers, friends, and family members' etcetera.
It is especially designed to be pondered upon mostly by you. For a complete 24 hours deep thought on each subject should be pondered upon. The reason being is to see how these guidelines could be implemented into your current life, how should they have been implemented in your past life, and how can they benefit your future.

It
is only through the true
belief
and usage of these
guidelines
that your life's
works will be greatly
affected
in its progress.

1

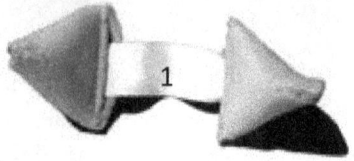

*In
life
you
have
to
embrace
the
positive
and
ignore
the
negative*

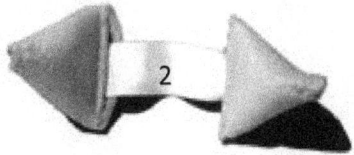

Within every unfortunate circumstance that arises in your life; there are hidden advantages that can turn you into a better person, but you just have to find them

*When your time
is
running-out,
you
cannot
afford to
make
not even
the
simplest
of
mistakes*

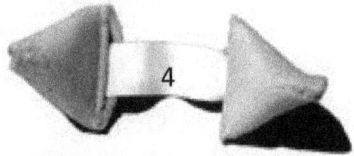

Be aware that
when
you wear a
mask for too
long
you begin
to forget
who
you originally
are
beneath
that mask

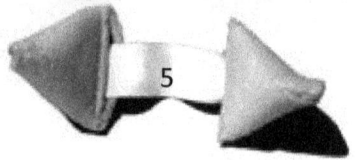

*In order to
win;
at
some point
you are
going
to
have to
believe
that you
can
win*

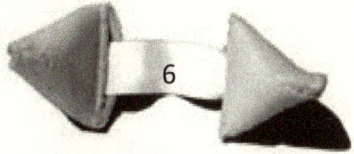

*When you
make
your
own
choices
you
have
to
pay
your
own
prices*

In a puzzling situation, everyone can benefit from a knew set of eyes, do not be ashamed to seek advise

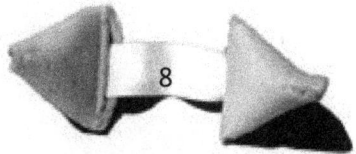

When there are worst-options to pick from, the bad-options don't seem that bad anymore

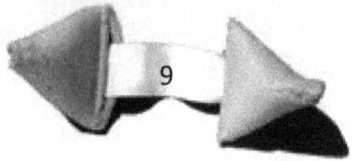

*You may be
able to
manipulate
but
you will
never
be able
to
really-control
what someone
else
truly-thinks*

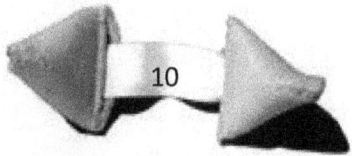

*For the
new-things
that you want
in your
life,
you are going
to have to
make room for
them by
canceling out
some of the
old-things*

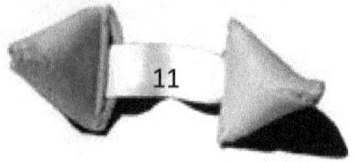

When you want to succeed in anything, you have to be willing to take a chance

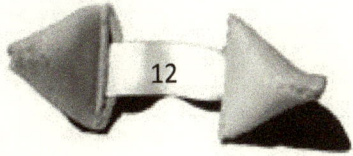

*In
order
for
you
to
rebuild
you
must
deconstruct*

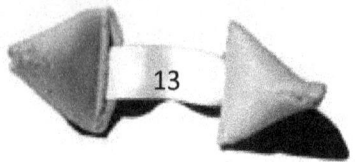

*Through
determination,
is how
the
challenges
that will
arise
in
your
life
be
solved*

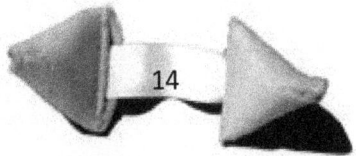

*Sometimes you
have to go
back
to the
beginning,
in essence
of
reflecting,
in order
to catch all
your
mistakes*

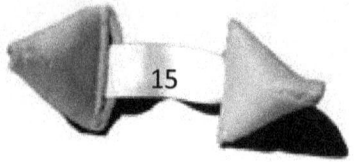

Never take

a

job

that

you

cannot

complete,

avoid

setting yourself

up

for

failure

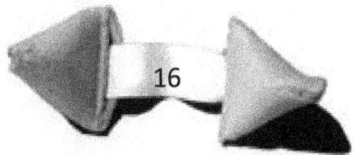

You need to become an editor in your life and cut out all the things that will not help you in accomplishing a focusing position towards your goal

*The answer
to 99
out of
100 percent
of
the problems
that you will
encounter in
your lifetime
can usually be
answered with
money*

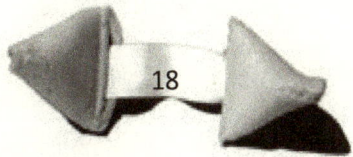

*Without
the bitter
that you
have
experienced
in your life
the
sweet
wouldn't
be
so
sweet*

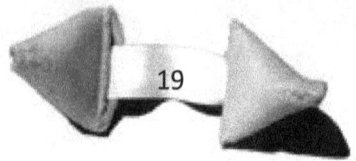

The
true-freedom
that you will
receive
from obtaining
total
independence
will
require
sacrifice
and
pain

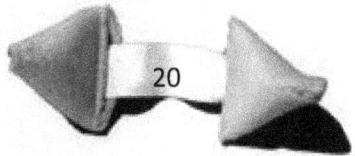

*There
aren't
any
coincidences
in
life
only
the
illusion
of
coincidences*

*When you begin
to notice that
people
do not want to
comprehend,
then that is
the
sign for you
to get
away
from that
situation*

*Sometimes
the only
mistake
that you make
is
assuming that
the
other
person
won't make
a
mistake*

*In life
there are some
very
nice citizens
and then
there are
some
very nasty
ones
but they all
appear first as
citizens*

*There
are
no
excuses
in
success*

*The
life
that you
want
is
something
that you
must
claim,
in order
to
receive-it*

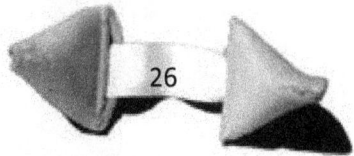

*To have a
plan
and
complete
it;
is
the
only
way to achieve
success
in
that endeavor*

*You
cannot
blame
anyone-else
for
something
that
you
have
done*

*When an idea
doesn't leave
and it sticks
with you for a
long-time;
then that
is a sign from
the universe,
telling you
that this is the
way
you must go*

*In life
you should
always
be
looking
to put
yourself
into a
position
where you
can use your
smarts*

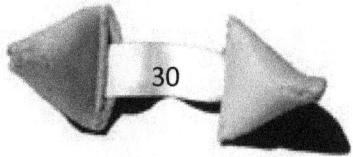

*In
order
to
be
successful
in
business
you
have
to
brand
yourself*

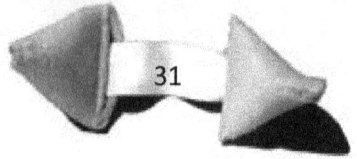

*A
stress
in your
personal
life
can and
will
bleed
into
your
business
life*

It's important to
acquire
the
key-pieces to a
project first
because
once you do,
everything
else will
fall
into its
place

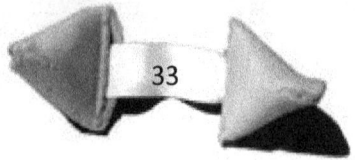

When you are not getting where you want to go by continuously doing what you are currently doing, you must wake-up to the fact that you're going to have to do things differently

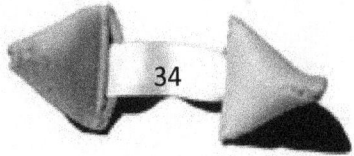

*A
chance
must
be
taken;
it is
not
something
that
you can
wait
for*

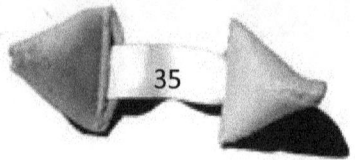

*The more
odds
that you stack
in your
favor
is the more of a
chance
that you will
have
of
accomplishing
your goal*

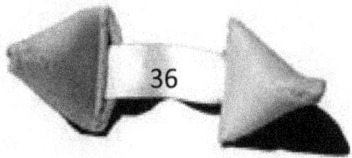

In a team; it doesn't matter what kind of disagreements that you may have, as long as that you are always doing what is right for the team

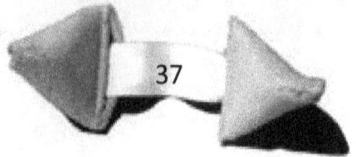

*A spouse needs
security,
which
is
something
you have
to
provide
or you will no
longer have
that
spouse*

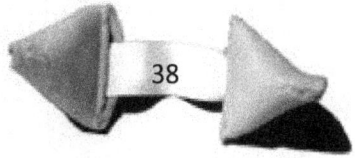

*What
you do not
want to
hear
is most likely
what
you
need
to
hear;
the
most*

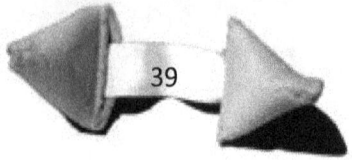

*A
little-problem
will
usually
escalate
into a
bigger-problem
when
you do not
attend
to it
immediately*

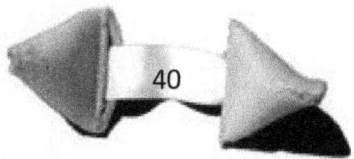

*Do
not
ever
let
your
emotions
over
rule
your
intelligence*

*Most
people
are
willing
to
meet
you
half-way,
if
you
let
them*

*In life you need
to know
where
you are going
and
also
what steps
that you
need to
take
to get
you there*

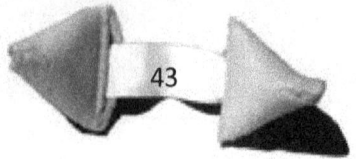

*Simpler is
always
less
complicated
and more
efficient which
leads
it
to being one of
the best ways
of how to do
a thing*

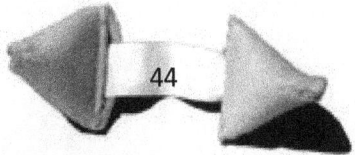

*You might
fall
going in the
right-direction
but
as long as
you can pick
yourself up
after you have
fallen and keep
on going, you
will get there*

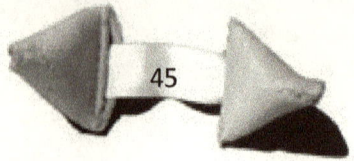

*Being
accurate
in
anything
that you do
will
save
you
the most
amount
of
time*

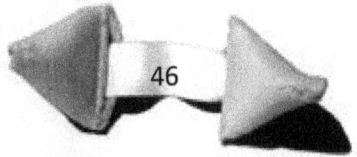

Avoid absorbing any aspects of a single minded persons attributes because to have one point of view on anything can be misleading

*When you are
going to take
any risk;
always make
sure
before you take
that
risk,
that the
pay-off
will be
worth it*

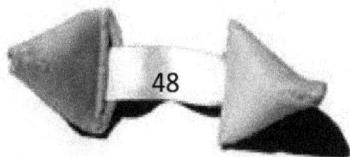

*When
you
think
big,
big-things
will
happen*

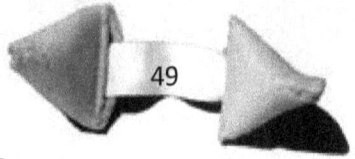

You never end a journey the same person you started-out the journey as

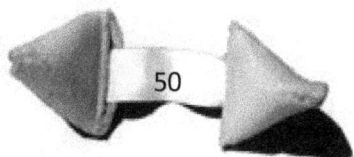

*It
takes
a
person
of
vision
to
do
something
great*

*Life
is
too
short
to
over
concern
yourself
with
the
small
stuff*

*Being given
the
opportunity
to
fail
is the
best
opportunity
you will
ever
be
given*

You have to take full-advantage of your resources, that is the reason why you have earned them

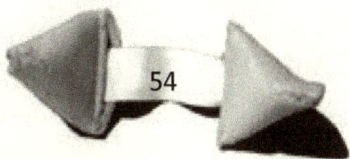

*When
you
have
a
certain
talent,
do
not
be
afraid
to
express-it*

*Your
expectation
of
victory
is
more
than
half
your
battle-won*

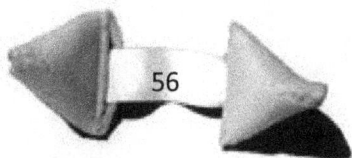

*You cannot
depend on the
will
of others
to make your
dreams
come-true, you
have to
follow-through
for yourself to
make your
dreams-happen*

You have to be active; your life-span is too short to sit around and wait for things to happen, you have to go out and make them happen

Your life will start to add-up to a painted-picture, how beautiful, mundane, or ugly that picture becomes is up to you

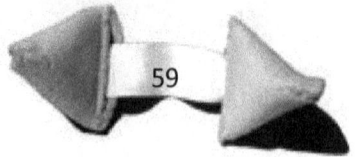

*In life you do
not have to be
the big-rudder;
however
you can be the
small-rudder
that turns the
big-rudder,
which turns
the
entire
ship*

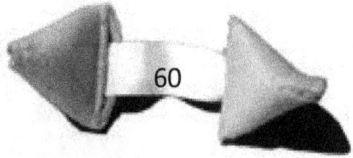

*It's important
to
understand
that no matter
how many
times you fall-
down; as long
as you get
back-up,
you still can
achieve your
dreams*

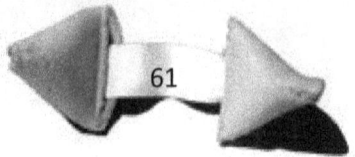

You have to
learn to do
things for
yourself
and not to
depend-on
others,
they may
not
move at the
same pace as
you

*Be someone
that has
chosen
their
living
and
not their
living
being
chosen
for
them*

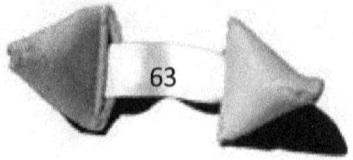

*Keep
in
mind
that in
life
everything
depends
on
the
reasoning's
behind
it*

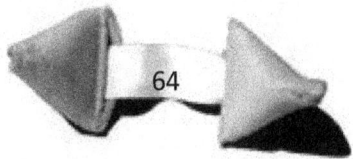

*You
cannot
forget
the
big-picture,
it is
what is
truly
important
in
your
life*

*Know
and
respect
your plan,
and
you will
not make
any
mistakes
in
regards
to it*

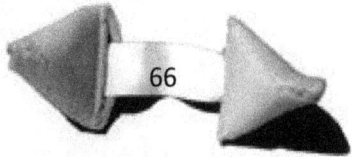

*It would take
a lot
more-time
for you to
ask
for things,
rather
than
for you
to go out
and
get them*

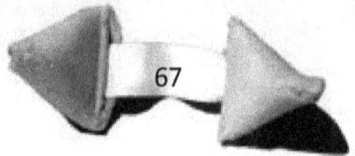

*The
best
revenge
that
you
can
ever
get;
is
to
win*

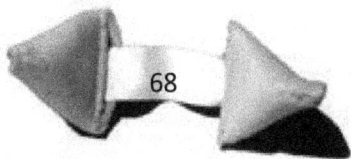

*Once you have
trained your
mind to focus on
the task
at hand and too
not allow
anything to
distract you
from your
goals,
everything
becomes
possible*

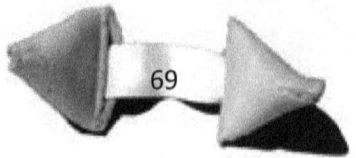

*When you don't
allow
fear to lead
you,
life
becomes
simple
you make
choices
and
never
look-back*

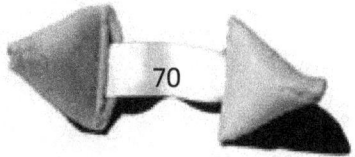

*There is no
need or time
to
wait,
you can
become
or
start becoming
what you
want
to be
right now*

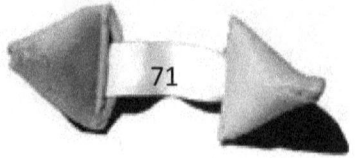

*Anything that
has any
meaning
isn't going to be
easy to
accomplish
but it will be
completely
worth
accomplishing it
because it
has
meaning*

*As a
progressive
human-being
it
is
your
duty
to
rise-up
to a
higher
playing-field*

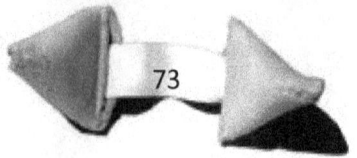

*Most times
it
doesn't
take much
for a
dramatic
change to
happen
when
success
is at
your feet*

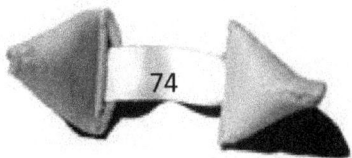

*The
harder-thing
to do and the
right-thing
to do
are
usually
the
same
thing
to
do*

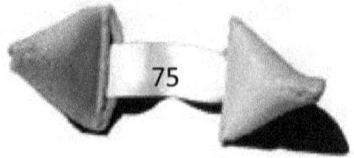

*Do not
give-up
and
gradually
everything
will
begin
to
make
sense*

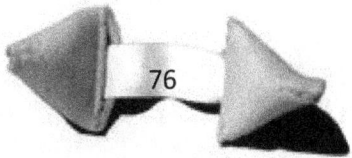

*It is extremely
important
to
follow
through
because
you
never really
know where
your
choices will
lead you*

*To acquire
anything
out of life
that is going
to be worth any
kind of
substantial
value,
you are going to
have to make
a few
sacrifices*

*Understand the
fact that you
can not
just follow
your
dreams;
if you want
to
catch them,
you
have to
chase-them*

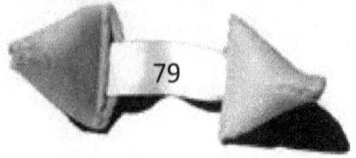

When you see
something
that
you want
and
it's worth
having, in order
to receive it
you are going to
have to
go
after it

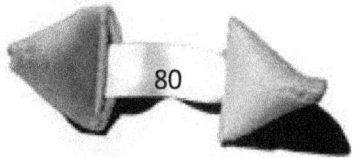

Learn the fact that you can always turn your stumbling blocks into stepping stones, and you will always be winning throughout life

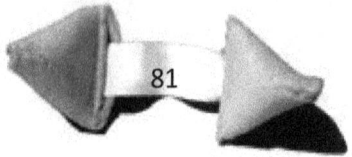

*It is very-wise
to
understand
that; what was
once a plus in
your life can
turn into a
negative and
once it does,
that negative
needs to be
eliminated*

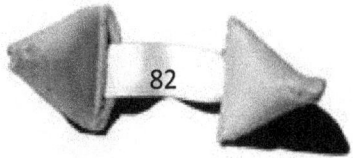

*In most things;
money will do
the
most amount of
talking for you
and the
heavier
it is the
louder
it
will be
heard*

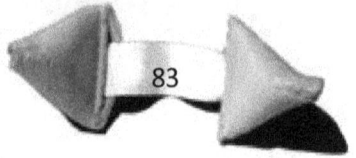

*In
whatever it is
that you are
involved
with, the
way
that
you
think
makes a
huge
difference*

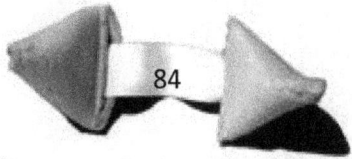

At
some-point
you are
going to
have to
take
a
risk
in order
to
get
ahead

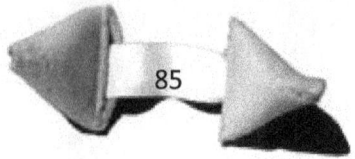

*What seems
like a
small-decision
to you
could be the
very
reason
why you make
all
the
rest of your
decisions*

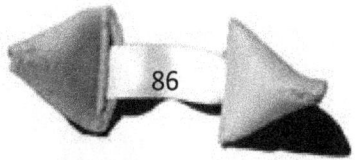

*In life you
don't
always
get
the
best-shot,
that is why
it is
so important to
take the
one that you
have*

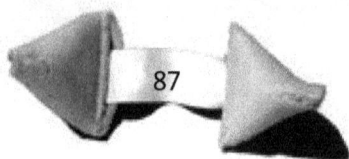

*It
is good to
always
keep in
mind
that
your
best-friend
isn't
everyone
else's
best-friend*

*Your
job in
life
is
to
become
as
amazing
as
you
can
become*

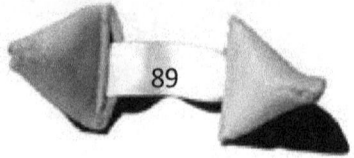

*Dreams are the
things that
must be
worked-on
and
if you are not
working on
your
dreams,
all they become
are
disappointments*

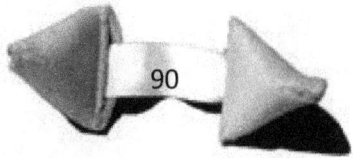

*In life you
have
to be
extremely
careful
with
the
things
that
you
don't
understand*

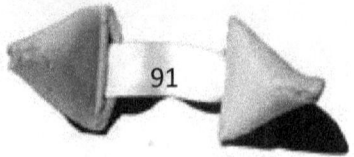

Sometimes we
become so
focused
with
our
enemies
that we
forget to
watch
those that we
consider our
friends

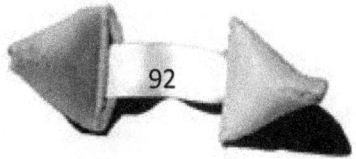

Sometimes the most important questions are the ones that you decide not to ask

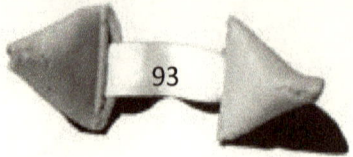

When you want
something
in
life, it is
important to
understand
that you
might not
get it
unless
you change
for it

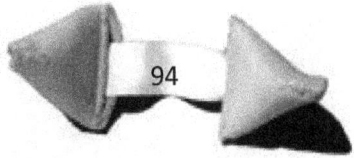

Every step that you make, should move you closer to the desired outcome of what you want your life to become or else why are you taking those steps

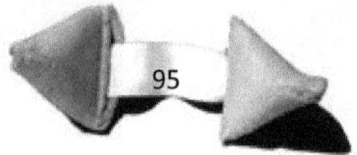

*The
person that
is
hated
by
everyone
knows
exactly
who
their
true-friends
are*

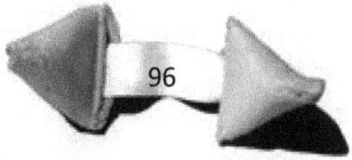

When
you go out on a
limb
and take a
risk
you're going to
have some
people that like
it
and some
people that
don't

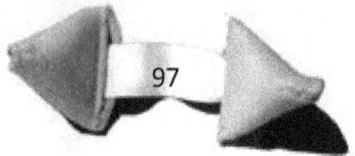

*When
you really
want to know
who a person is
close to, just
look at who
they share both
their bad
and
good
news
with*

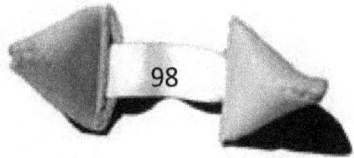

There
is
no
true
failure
in
the
efforts
of
trying

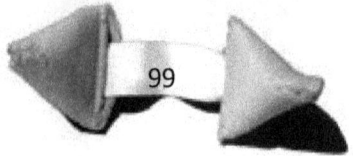

*Never
doubt
your
minds-intuition,
it
will
keep you
out
of
a lot
of
trouble*

Just because you can; does not mean that you should

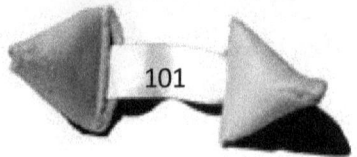

*Every passing
minute
is
another
chance
to turn
your
situation
around
into
something
fantastic*

*You should
always
go
with
the
best
idea
that
you have;
all
the
time*

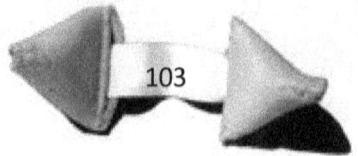

*The
opportunity
to move
another level
upward,
is what
you
should
always
be
looking
for*

When you receive an opportunity to become better today, that opportunity should not be taken lightly

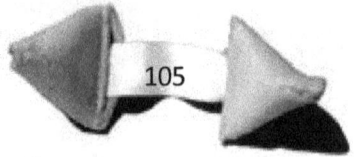

*The only way
to become
truly-free
is by
obtaining
the
type
of success
that will give
you
total
independence*

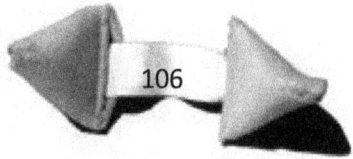

*Motivation
is
the
gas
that
will
allow
you
to
complete
your
task*

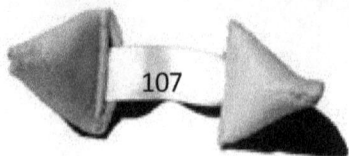

*At
the point
of
deception
is where
you need
to
calculate
what you
do
not
know*

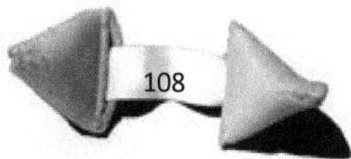

*When
a
problem
occurs;
it is to
late
to be
sorry,
just
fix
the
problem*

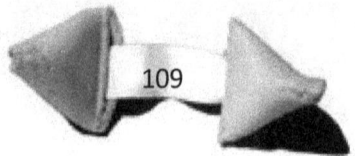

*In life; in order
to
better
yourself,
you
have to learn
how to
change
whether
you want to
or
not*

*To really make
certain things
work,
your time
and
effort
has
to
be
given
to
it*

111

*Always
stay
prepared
because
the
universe
doesn't
ask if
your
ready
or
not*

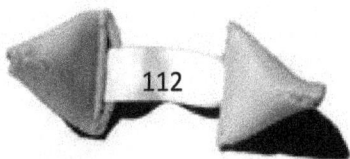

*No matter
what
position
you're
in,
you
should
always
try
to
better
yourself*

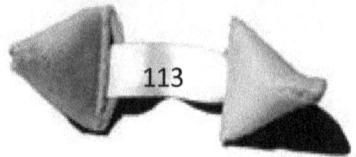

*In whatever
that
you plan to do;
you
have to
stick with
your efforts
towards it,
in
order
to
accomplish-it*

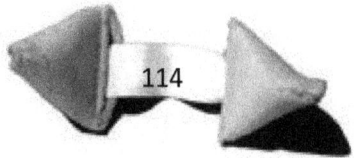

*In
life
you
can not
get
better
until
you
acknowledge
your
mistakes*

When you are trying to improve by advancing to new higher levels, it is important to understand that you will never change your destination by staying the same course

*Life
is too short
to
spend time
with the
people
that are
not
worthy
of
spending your
time with*

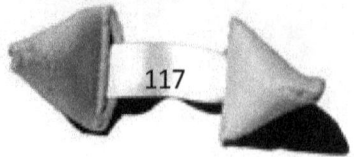

*You have to
shed
some
of
your
past
experiences
in order
to
move on
and
grow*

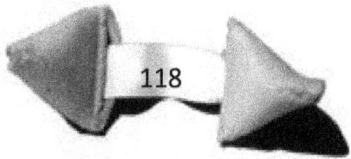

Remember
that your
breath
is a
clock
that is
ticking
and
your
time
does
run-out

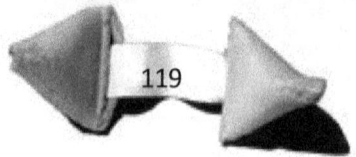

*It's important
for you to
realize
that your
mental-attitude
is
what
is the
driving-force
behind
everything
that you do*

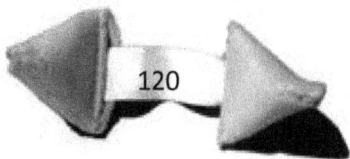

*You have to
have a
plan,
without a
plan
you are
doomed
to a life
of the
cattle
just waiting
to be herded*

*When
they've
never
heard-of
you,
people
judge
at
first
by
your
appearance*

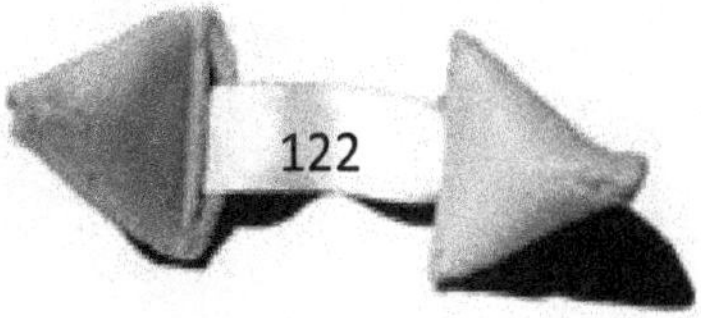

*A
deadline
has
a
way
of
focusing
the
mind*

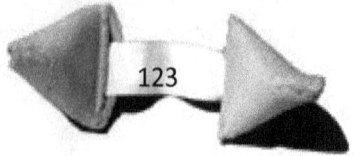

*Learn how
to
place
yourself
into
positions
where
opportunity
can
see
you*

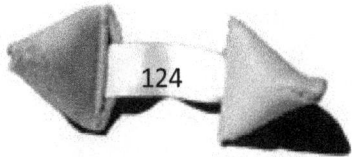

*What
you want
and
what you
can afford
might be
two
different
things,
learn
the
difference*

*Just
because
you
face
adversity
does not
mean
that
you
have
to
give-up*

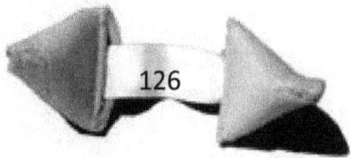

*Use your
ideas;
there is
no-sense
in
having
them if you
are not
going
to
use
them*

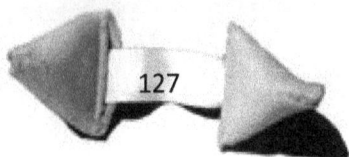

*The
more
sophisticated
the
game,
the
more
sophisticated
the
opponent*

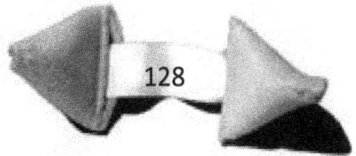

*In life
in order
to
succeed
in
a
great-way
you
have
to
have
vision*

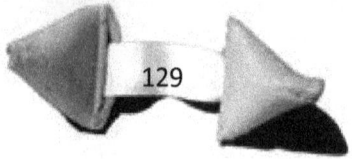

*It is an
extremely
important rule
that
when you are
going for
success;
that you have
to go where
ever the
opportunities
take you*

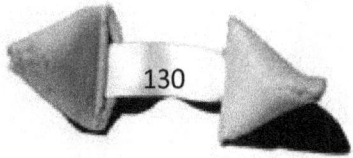

*The pocket
that you
think
you're in,
isn't
always
the
pocket
that
you
are
in*

*The more
risk
that you
take
the more
of
a
reward
you
tend
to
make*

*Work to your
strengths
and
improve
your
weaknesses
while you are
waiting
for your
plans
to run their
course*

You
have to
look
behind the
words
in
order
to
get
the
full
meaning

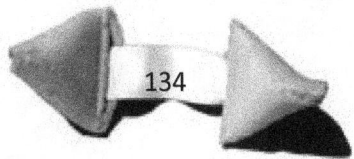

*Edit
yourself
to
where
everything
that
is
left
is
perfect*

*In
order
to
be
successful
you
have
to
take
some
risk*

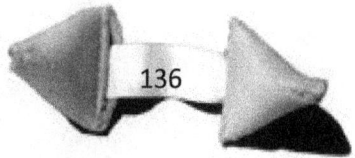

*All that
really matters
in
life
is for you to
know
what you
really want
and
then for you to
go
after it*

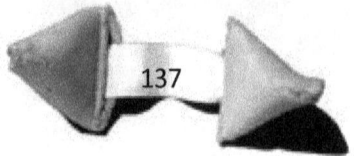

Sometimes
in life
all
that
you
have
is
what
you
are
going
after

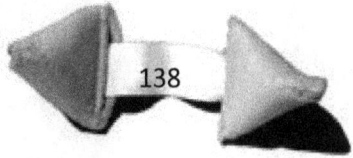

*There
are
repercussions
in
life
for
not
censoring
yourself*

*In life your
supposed to
learn how to
take the lessons
that you have
learnt
and use them
to move
forward; your
supposed to use
them to move
on to
greater-success*

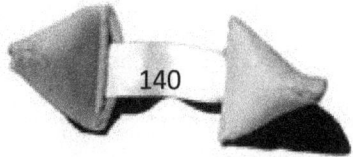

*Plenty of people
use
excuses;
if you want
to
become
successful,
make
sure that
you are not one
of
them*

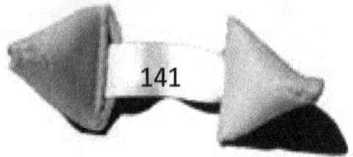

Upon being truthful, one's body-language should match the message

*When
your
response
is
confident,
it
will
always
put
people
more at
ease*

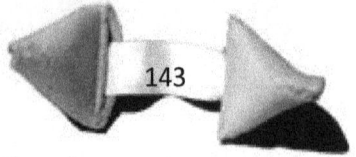

Not doing things in a rush, allows for newer and greater-ideas to settle-in and enhance the original-task

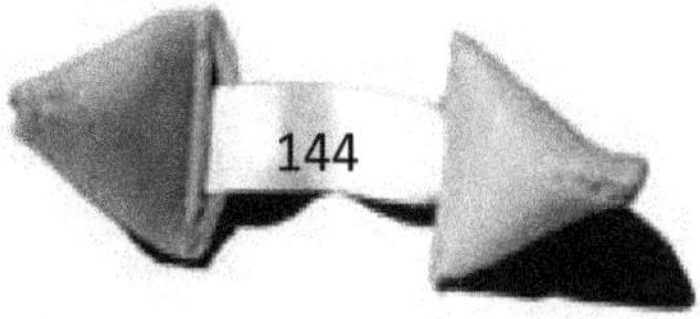

*Obvious
answers
are
usually
the
right
ones*

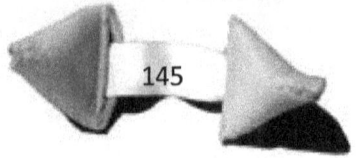

When you want different-results from the ones that you are currently receiving, you are going to have to choose a different-route

It is important
for you
to
realize
that the
money
that
you
acquire
guaranties
your
stability

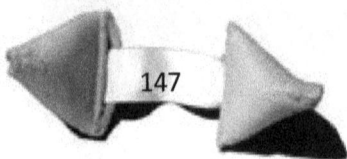

*You should
never
be
ashamed
of
your
abilities,
they
are
yours
to be
expressed*

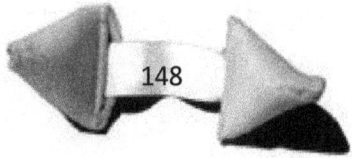

You have to dig the worms when you want to catch the fish

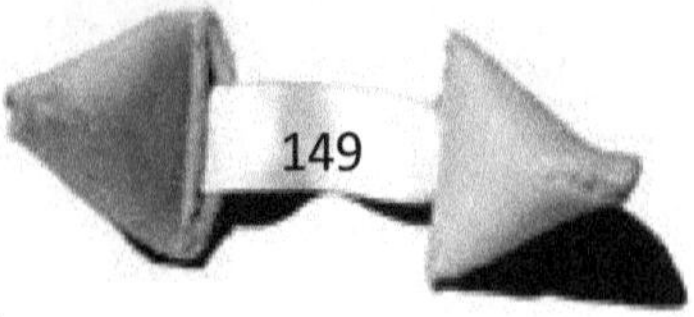

*The
best
way
to
get-over
the
past,
is
to
start
something
new*

Greed is a very hard emotion to put into check and it will definitely hurt you in the end, you should want absolutely nothing to do with it

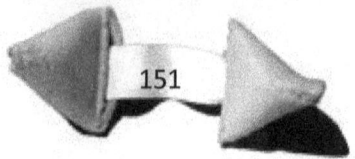

There
can come that
day
when you
wish
you had
done
that
little-bit-of-evil
for
that
greater-good

*Sometimes
it's
not
important
which
way
that you
jump,
just
that
you
jump*

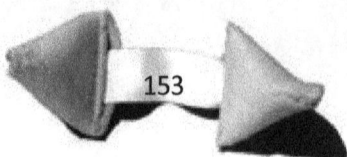

*Be extremely
wary
of the
picture
that you are
creating
for
yourself
because it will
eventually
be
filled*

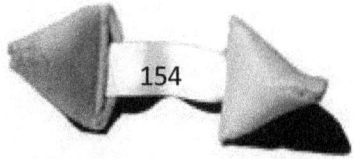

When trying to
turn the
equivalent of a
big-ship
around,
just remember
that it cannot
be turned in an
instant it takes
a while
to
change

It's important to your success to keep in mind that you do have the right to remove yourself from any situation that does not suite you

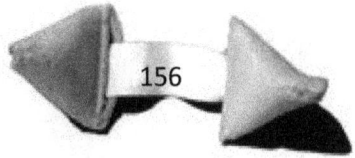

Do not take
your eye
off of the
target
and you
will
achieve
success
in
accomplishing
your
objective

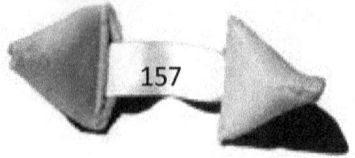

*You can never
become
any
bigger
than
how
big
you
think
you
can
become*

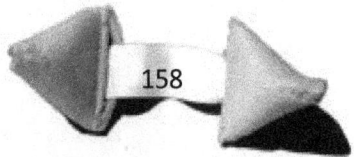

*Sometimes
risking
everything
will be
the
only
choice
you
have
in order to
get
ahead*

The end

Additional books written by
Dr. Kareem Pottinger available online at
www.FORTUNECOOKIES.me
and your local book stores nationwide

<u>FORTUNE COOKIES VOLUMES 1-11</u>

   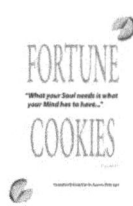

also   available   on   your

<u>Kindle</u>   <u>Nook</u>   <u>Apple</u>   <u>devices</u>

  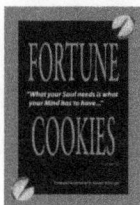

www.ingramcontent.com/pod-product-compliance
Lightning Source LLC
Chambersburg PA
CBHW030104070426
42448CB00037B/964